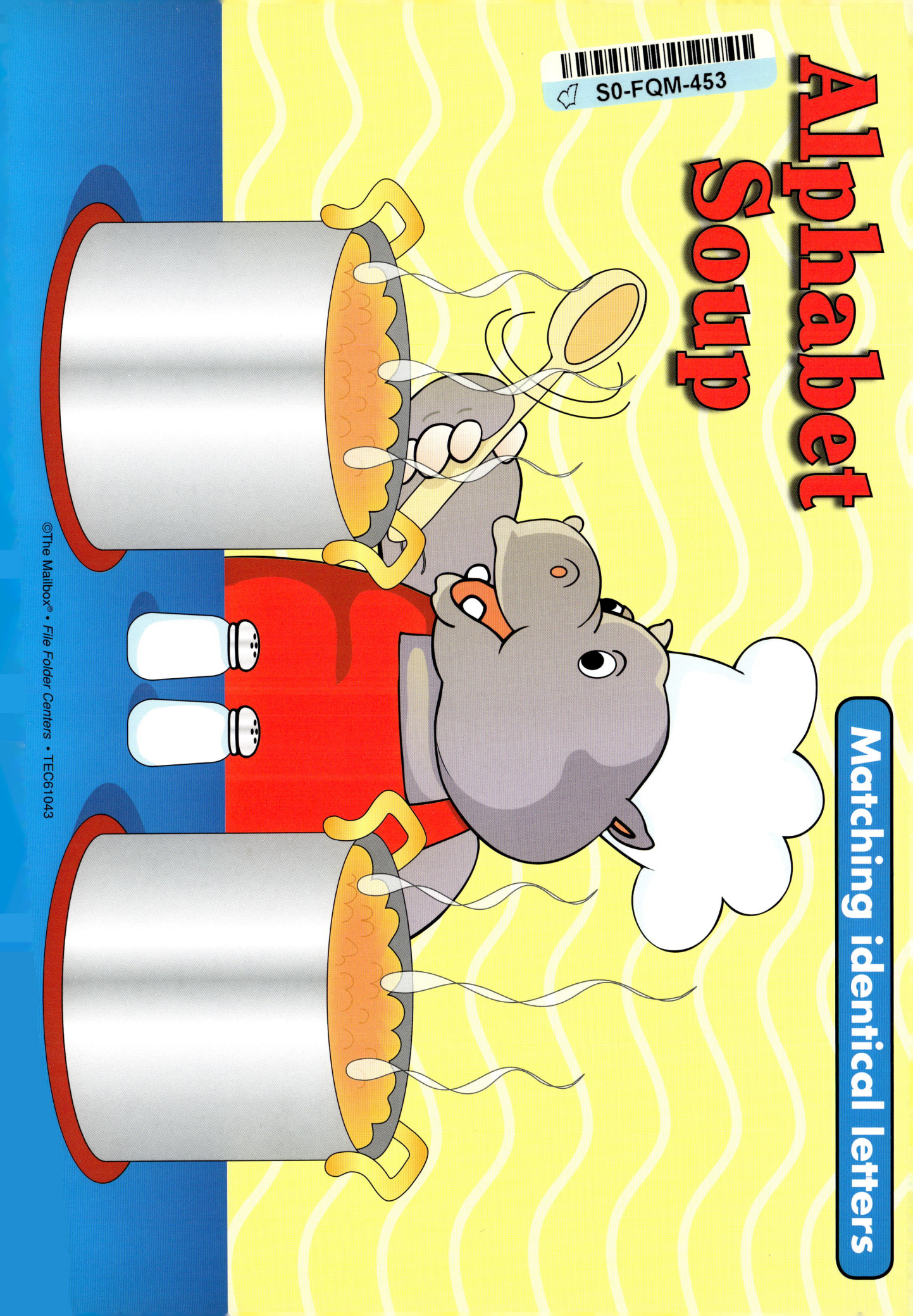

Alphabet Soup

Matching identical letters

©The Mailbox® • File Folder Centers • TEC61043

Match.
Place.

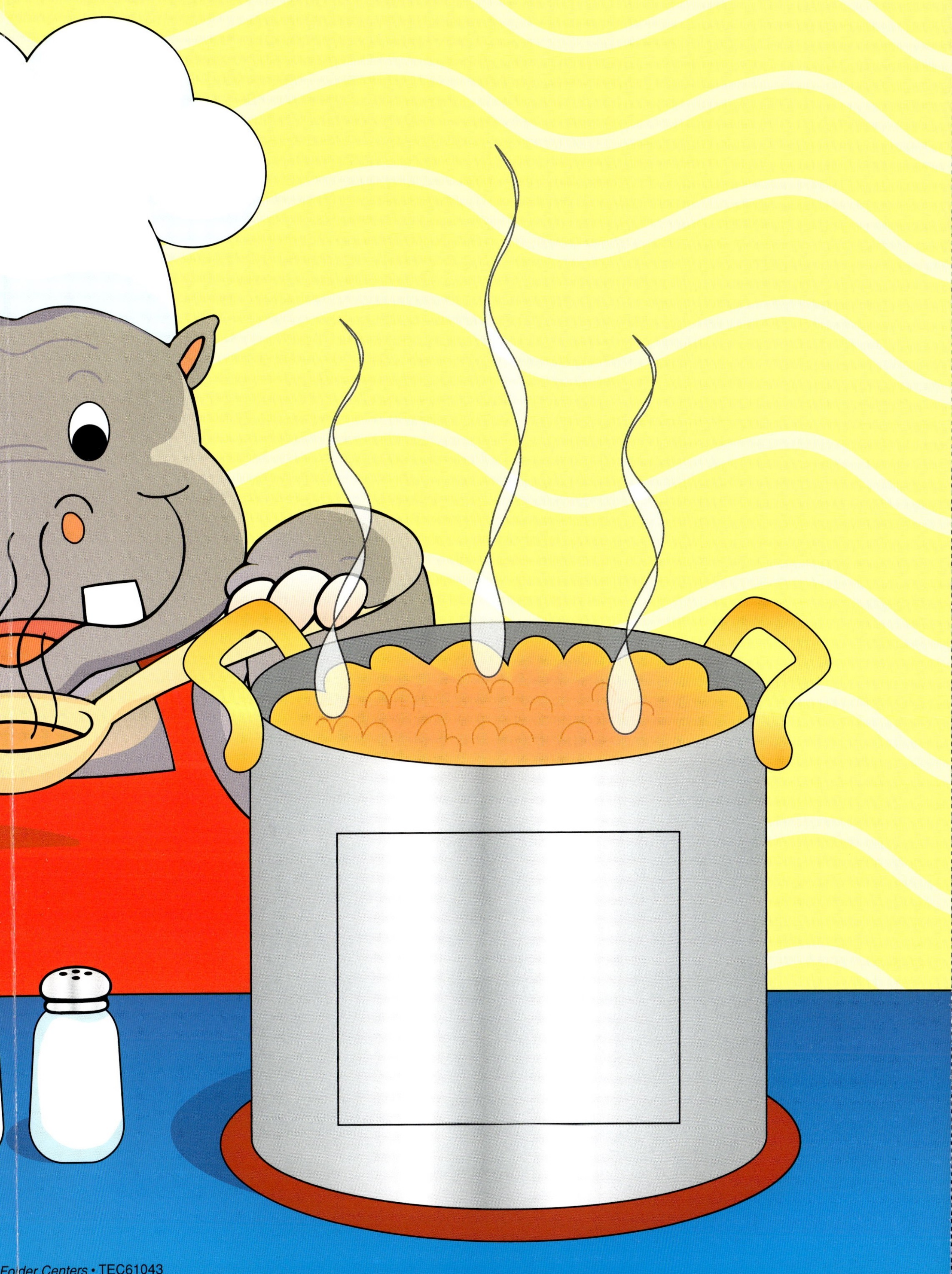

Alphabet Soup

Matching identical letters

Inside this folder:

Match.
Place.

To find the **cards** for this center, see page 55.

To find the **teacher page** and **take-home practice page,** see pages 27 and 28.

Turn to see the front of the folder.

THE MAILBOX

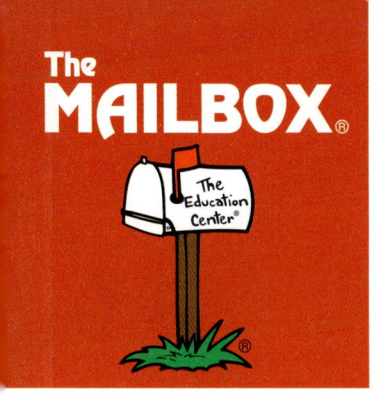

MATH & LITERACY

12 File Folder Centers

grade PreK

- Counting to 5; counting to 10
- Matching one to one
- Sorting by color
- Ordering by size
- Copying simple patterns
- Sorting shapes
- Identifying rhyming pictures
- More identifying rhyming pictures
- Beginning sound /s/
- Beginning sound /m/
- Beginning sound /f/
- Matching identical letters

Managing Editor: Kimberly Brugger-Murphy

Editorial Team: Becky S. Andrews, Kimberley Bruck, Karen P. Shelton, Diane Badden, Thad H. McLaurin, Sharon Murphy, Lynn Drolet, Kelly Robertson, Karen A. Brudnak, Hope Rodgers, Dorothy C. McKinney

Production Team: Lori Z. Henry, Pam Crane, Rebecca Saunders, Jennifer Tipton Cappoen, Chris Curry, Sarah Foreman, Theresa Lewis Goode, Clint Moore, Greg D. Rieves, Barry Slate, Donna K. Teal, Zane Williard, Tazmen Carlisle, Marsha Heim, Lynette Dickerson, Mark Rainey

www.themailbox.com

©2006 The Mailbox®
All rights reserved.
ISBN10 #156234714-4 • ISBN13 #978-156234-714-7

Except as provided for herein, no part of this publication may be reproduced or transmitted in any form or by any means, electronic or mechanical, including photocopying, recording, or storing in any information storage and retrieval system or electronic online bulletin board, without prior written permission from The Education Center, Inc. Permission is given to the original purchaser to reproduce patterns and reproducibles for individual classroom use only and not for resale or distribution. Reproduction for an entire school or school system is prohibited. Please direct written inquiries to The Education Center, Inc., P.O. Box 9753, Greensboro, NC 27429-0753. The Education Center®, The Mailbox®, the mailbox/post/grass logo, and The Mailbox Book Company® are registered trademarks of The Education Center, Inc. All other brand or product names are trademarks or registered trademarks of their respective companies.

Manufactured in China

Table of Contents

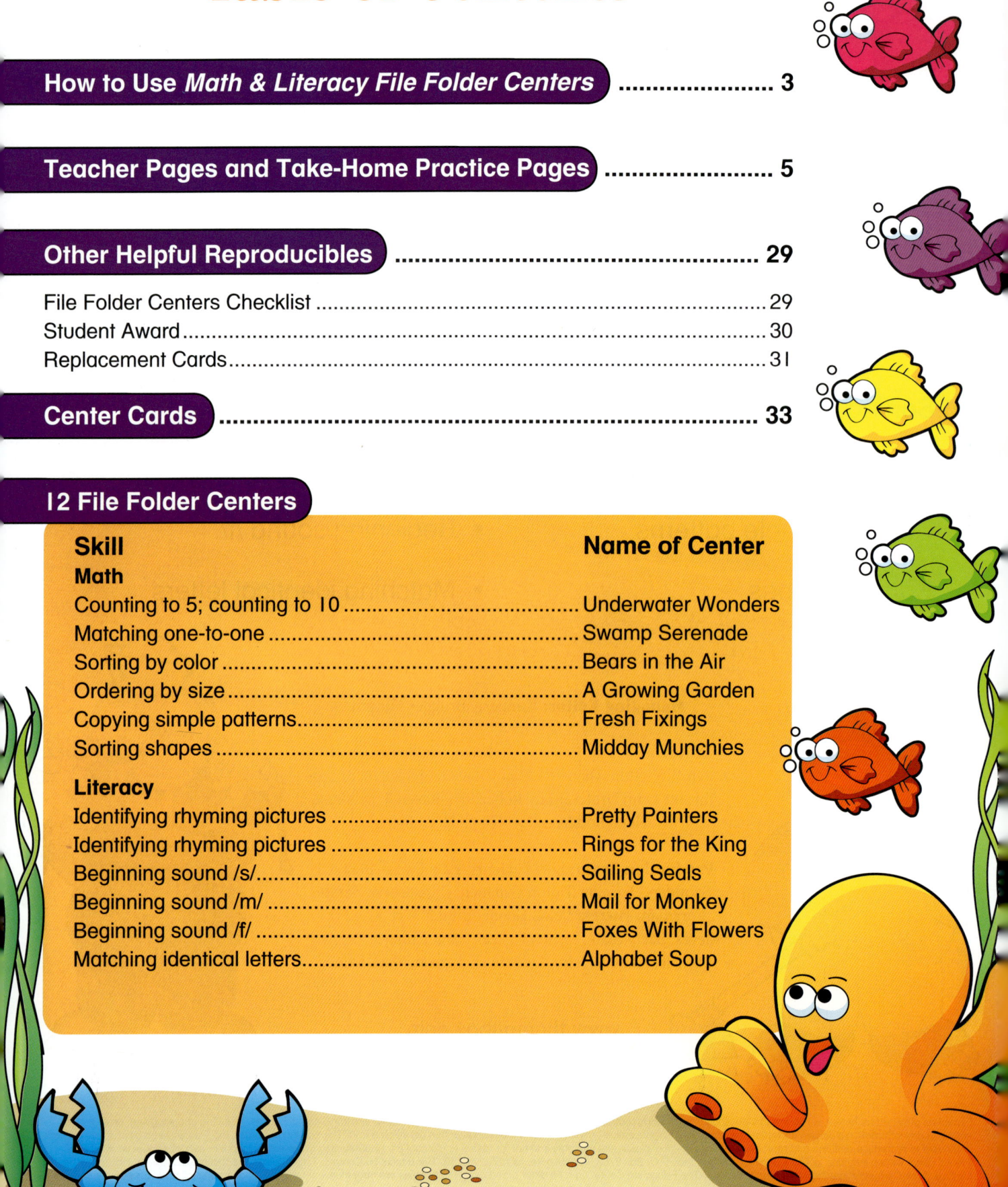

How to Use *Math & Literacy File Folder Centers* 3

Teacher Pages and Take-Home Practice Pages 5

Other Helpful Reproducibles 29
File Folder Centers Checklist 29
Student Award 30
Replacement Cards 31

Center Cards 33

12 File Folder Centers

Skill	Name of Center
Math	
Counting to 5; counting to 10	Underwater Wonders
Matching one-to-one	Swamp Serenade
Sorting by color	Bears in the Air
Ordering by size	A Growing Garden
Copying simple patterns	Fresh Fixings
Sorting shapes	Midday Munchies
Literacy	
Identifying rhyming pictures	Pretty Painters
Identifying rhyming pictures	Rings for the King
Beginning sound /s/	Sailing Seals
Beginning sound /m/	Mail for Monkey
Beginning sound /f/	Foxes With Flowers
Matching identical letters	Alphabet Soup

How to Use

Math & Literacy File Folder Centers

1. Read the teacher page for each file folder center. Prepare each center as directed.
2. Use the center as directed on the teacher page to reinforce the corresponding skills you are teaching.
3. Provide more practice with a center's skill using the take-home practice page.

Teacher Page

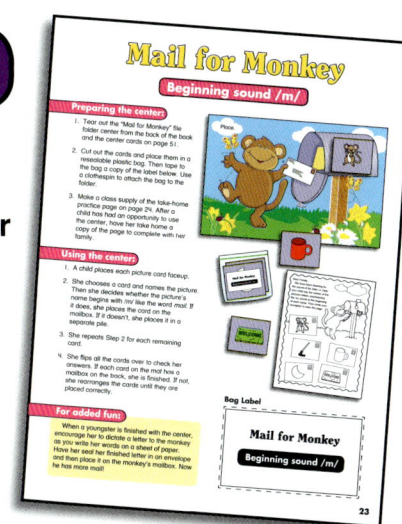

Targeted Math or Literacy Skill

File Folder Center

Reproducible Bag Label

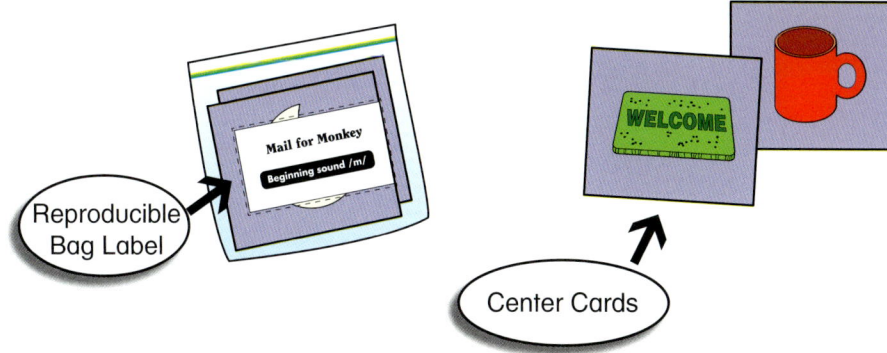

Center Cards

Take-Home Practice Page

Options
- Extend or enhance each center using the "For Added Fun" suggestions located at the bottom of each teacher page.
- Use the reproducible checklist on page 29 to track student progress.
- Encourage student progress with the award on page 30.

3

Underwater Wonders

Counting to 5; counting to 10

Preparing the center:

1. Tear out the "Underwater Wonders" file folder center from the back of the book and the center cards on page 33.

2. Cut out the cards. Place five or ten of the cards, depending on your children's ability, into a resealable plastic bag. Then tape to the bag a copy of the label below. Use a clothespin to attach the bag to the folder. (Color a copy of the cards on page 31 to use as replacements when needed.)

3. Make a class supply of the take-home practice page on page 6. After a child has had an opportunity to use the center, have him take home a copy of the page to complete with his family.

Using the center:

1. A child places each card faceup.

2. He counts the fish aloud as he places them in the water above the ship.

3. He counts the fish again, pointing to each one.

For added fun:

Place ten large coin cutouts in a decorative box to make a treasure chest. After a child completes the center as described above, explain that the ship on the page is a sunken pirate ship and you've found its hidden treasure chest. Encourage the child to open the chest and count the pieces of gold as he places them on the ship. It's a ten-piece treasure!

Bag Label

Underwater Wonders

Counting to 5; counting to 10

TEC61043

Dear Family,

We have been counting in preschool! Help your child count the fish shown. Then invite your youngster to color the page.

Swamp Serenade

Matching one to one

Preparing the center:

1. Tear out the "Swamp Serenade" file folder center from the back of the book and the frog cards on page 35.

2. Cut out the cards and place them in a resealable plastic bag. Then tape to the bag a copy of the label below. Use a clothespin to attach the bag to the folder. (Color a copy of the cards on page 31 to use as replacements when needed.)

3. Make a class supply of the take-home practice page on page 8. After a child has had an opportunity to use the center, have her take home a copy of the page to complete with her family.

Using the center:

1. A child places each card faceup.

2. She counts the number of frogs; then she counts the number of lily pads.

3. She places one frog on each lily pad.

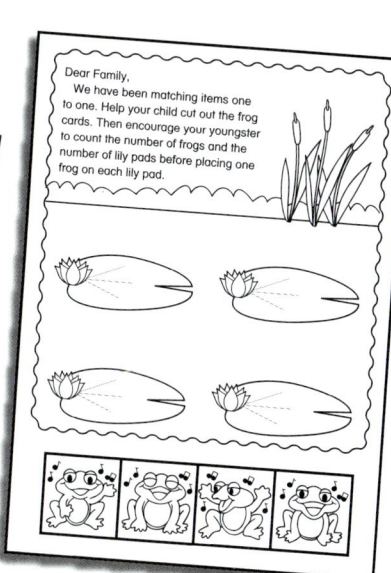

For added fun:

Nestle the frog cards in a container of blue crinkled paper shreds or blue-tinted rice (water). The child can then manipulate the frogs to "hop" out of the water before completing Steps 2 and 3 above.

Bag Label

Swamp Serenade

Matching one to one

TEC61043

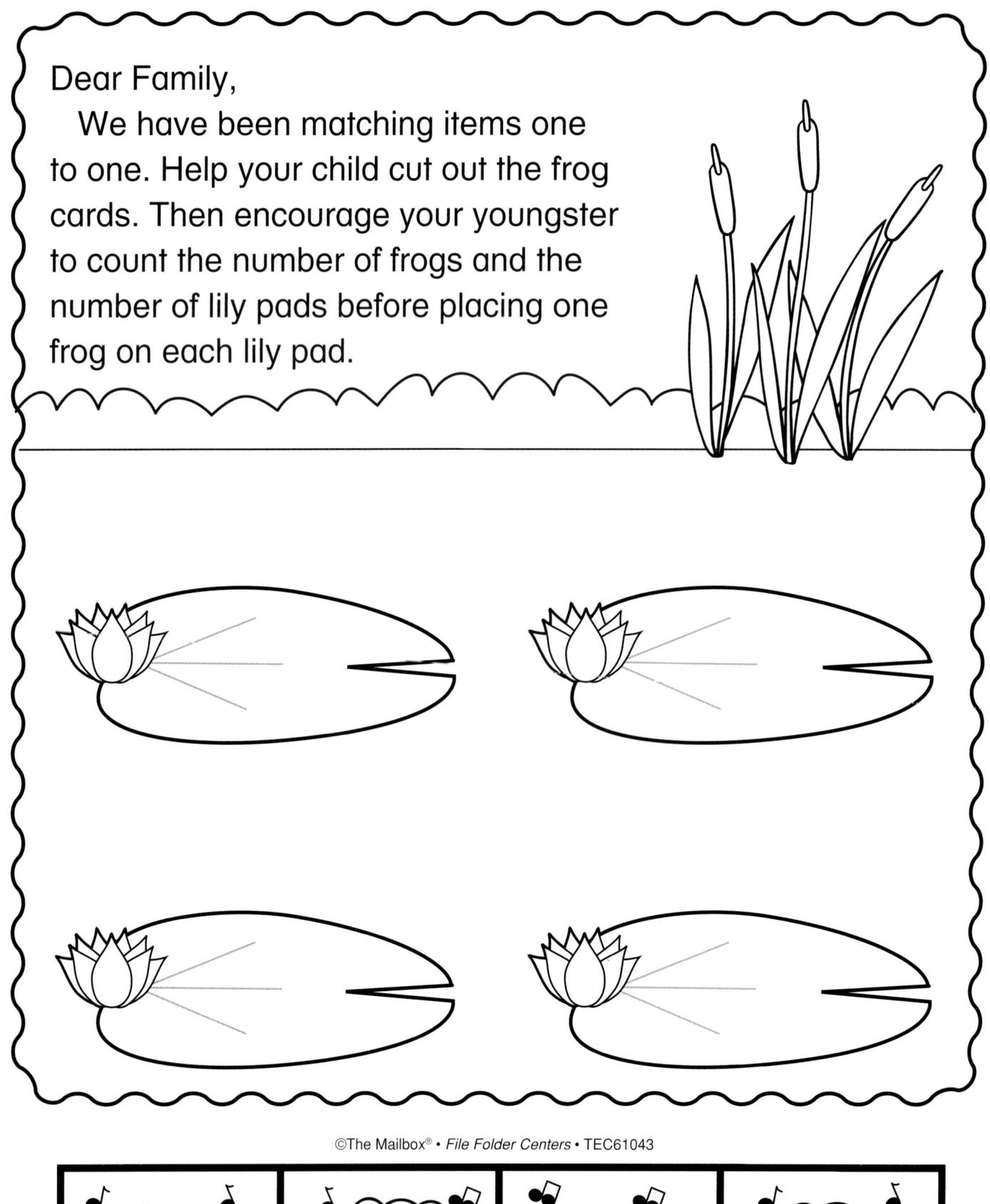

Dear Family,
  We have been matching items one to one. Help your child cut out the frog cards. Then encourage your youngster to count the number of frogs and the number of lily pads before placing one frog on each lily pad.

©The Mailbox® • *File Folder Centers* • TEC61043

TEC61043   TEC61043   TEC61043   TEC61043

Bears in the Air

Sorting by color

Preparing the center:

1. Tear out the "Bears in the Air" file folder center from the back of the book and the center cards on page 37.

2. Cut out the cards and place them in a resealable plastic bag. Then tape to the bag a copy of the label below. Use a clothespin to attach the bag to the folder. (Color a copy of the cards on page 31 to use as replacements when needed.)

3. Make a class supply of the take-home practice page on page 10. After a child has had an opportunity to use the center, have him take home a copy of the page to complete with his family.

Using the center:

1. A child places each card faceup.

2. He chooses a card and places it on the basket with the corresponding color.

3. He repeats Step 2 with each remaining card.

4. He flips over each stack of cards on the mat. If the cards in each stack show identical pictures, he is finished. If not, he rearranges the cards until they are placed correctly.

For added fun:

After the child has completed the center, explain that the bears on the mat brought a snack of fish—a common bear food—to nibble on while on their balloon ride. Tell the youngster that these generous bears decided to share some of their snack with him. Then reveal a small cup of Goldfish Colors crackers for him to snack on. Have him sort the fish by color and then eat them. Don't forget to thank the bears!

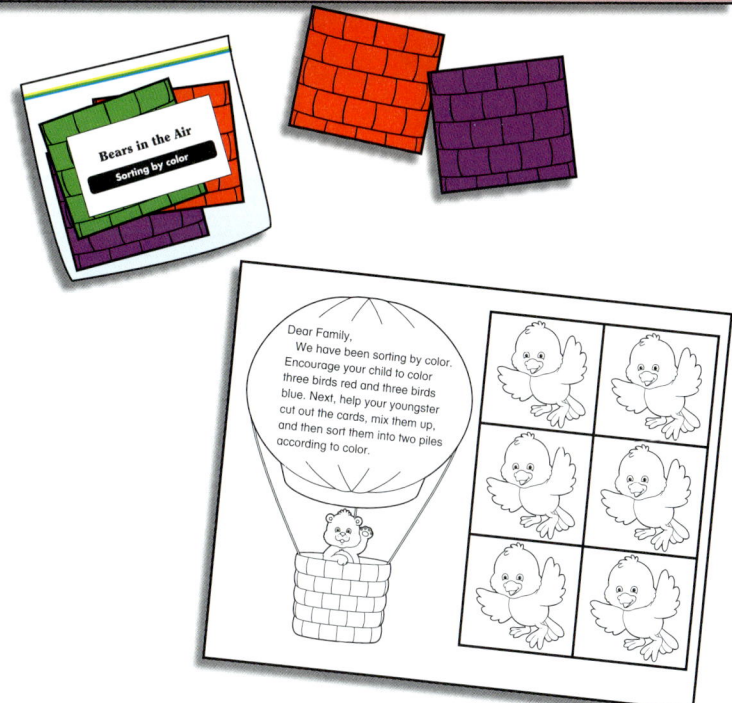

Bag Label

Bears in the Air

Sorting by color

TEC61043

Dear Family,
We have been sorting by color. Encourage your child to color three birds red and three birds blue. Next, help your youngster cut out the cards, mix them up, and then sort them into two piles according to color.

A Growing Garden

Ordering by size

Preparing the center:

1. Tear out the "A Growing Garden" file folder center from the back of the book and the center cards on page 39.

2. Cut out the cards and place them in a resealable plastic bag. Then tape to the bag a copy of the label below. Use a clothespin to attach the bag to the folder. (Color a copy of the cards on page 32 to use as replacements when needed.)

3. Make a class supply of the take-home practice page on page 12. After a child has had an opportunity to use the center, have him take home a copy of the page to complete with his family.

Using the center:

1. A child places each card faceup.

2. He chooses the cards for one type of flower. Then he arranges them in order by size on the center mat.

3. He flips all of the cards over to check his answers. If the numbers on the backs of the cards are in order, he places the cards in the bag. If the numbers aren't in order, he rearranges the cards until they are in the correct order; then he places the cards in the bag.

4. He repeats Steps 2 and 3 for the remaining set of cards.

For added fun:

To extend the center, trim the stems of four artificial flowers so that each one is a different length. Then, after the child has ordered both sets of cards, encourage him to order the artificial flowers as well.

Place.

Dear Family,
We have been ordering by size. Help your child cut out the cards and place them in a row from shortest to tallest.

Bag Label

A Growing Garden

Ordering by size

TEC61043

©The Mailbox® • File Folder Centers • TEC61043

Dear Family,
We have been ordering by size. Help your child cut out the cards and place them in a row from shortest to tallest.

Fresh Fixings

Copying simple patterns

Preparing the center:

1. Tear out the "Fresh Fixings" file folder center from the back of the book and the vegetable strips and cards on page 41.

2. Cut out the cards and place them in a resealable plastic bag. Then tape to the bag a copy of the label below. Use a clothespin to attach the bag to the folder. (Color a copy of the cards on page 32 to use as replacements when needed.)

3. Make a class supply of the take-home practice page on page 14. After a child has had an opportunity to use the center, have her take home a copy of the page to complete with her family.

Using the center:

1. A child places the strips and cards faceup.

2. She chooses a strip and places it on the mat. Then she reads the pattern from left to right, naming the colors or the names of the vegetables as she points to each one.

3. She copies the pattern by placing the matching cards below the strip.

4. She repeats Steps 2 and 3 for the remaining strip.

For added fun:

Place a salad bowl and a pair of salad tongs at the center along with a supply of red, orange, and green construction paper scraps. Each time the child places a card on the mat, encourage her to choose one of the scraps of paper, crumple it, and place it in the salad bowl. Once she's completed the center, invite her to use the salad tongs to toss her paper salad.

Bag Label

Fresh Fixings

Copying simple patterns

TEC61043

Dear Family,
We have been making simple patterns. Help your child choose two crayons in different colors. Then encourage your youngster to color the vegetables above, alternating colors to make a simple pattern.

©The Mailbox® • *File Folder Centers* • TEC61043

Midday Munchies

Sorting shapes

Preparing the center:

1. Tear out the "Midday Munchies" file folder center from the back of the book and the center cards on page 43.

2. Cut out the cards and place them in a resealable plastic bag. Then tape to the bag a copy of the label below. Use a clothespin to attach the bag to the folder.

3. Make a class supply of the take-home practice page on page 16. After a child has had an opportunity to use the center, have him take home a copy of the page to complete with his family.

Using the center:

1. A child places each card faceup.

2. She chooses a card and then places it on the mat over the matching shape.

3. She repeats Step 2 with each remaining card.

4. She flips all of the cards over to check her answers. If the cards from each stack have matching pictures, she is finished. If not, she rearranges the cards until they are placed correctly.

For added fun:

Use a black permanent marker to draw ants on a vinyl tablecloth. Place the tablecloth on the floor to resemble a picnic area. Then place the mat and cards on the tablecloth. Encourage a child to visit the picnic area to complete the center. When she is finished, invite her to nibble on a snack of crackers in a variety of shapes.

Bag Label

Midday Munchies

Sorting shapes

TEC61043

©The Mailbox® • *File Folder Centers* • TEC61043

Dear Family,
   We have been sorting shapes. Help your child cut out the cards and sort them into three piles according to shape.

©The Mailbox® • *File Folder Centers* • TEC61043

TEC61043

TEC61043

TEC61043

TEC61043

TEC61043

TEC61043

16

Pretty Painters

Identifying rhyming pictures

Preparing the center:

1. Tear out the "Pretty Painters" file folder center from the back of the book and the center cards on page 45.

2. Cut out the cards and place them in a resealable plastic bag. Then tape to the bag a copy of the label below. Use a clothespin to attach the bag to the folder.

3. Make a class supply of the take-home practice page on page 18. After a child has had an opportunity to use the center, have him take home a copy of the page to complete with his family.

Using the center:

1. A child places each card faceup.

2. He chooses a card. He says the word *can* and then the name of the picture on the card.

3. If the two words rhyme, he places the card on the paint can. If they don't, he places the card in a separate pile.

4. He repeats Steps 2 and 3 for each remaining card.

5. He flips all of the cards over to check his answers. If each card from the mat has a can on the back, he is finished. If not, he rearranges the cards until they are placed correctly.

For added fun:

When a student finishes the center, tell him that he is now an official painter. Give him a painter's brush and an empty container that resembles a paint can. Then encourage him to use his supplies and imagination to "paint" furniture and other objects nearby.

Bag Label

Pretty Painters
Identifying rhyming pictures

TEC61043

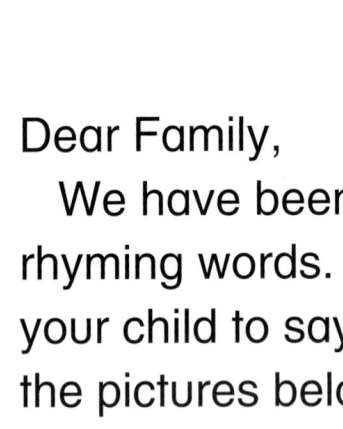

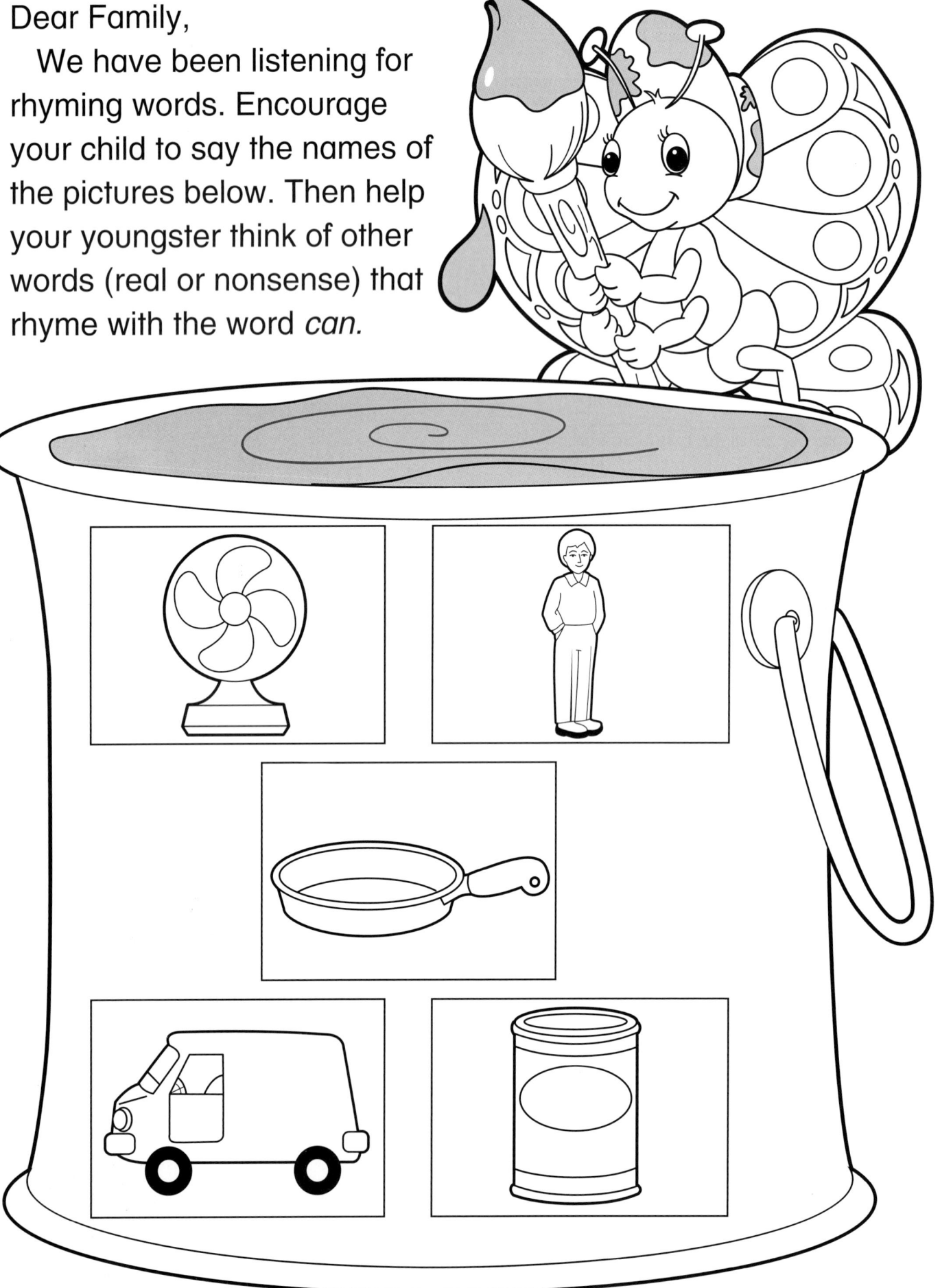

Dear Family,
   We have been listening for rhyming words. Encourage your child to say the names of the pictures below. Then help your youngster think of other words (real or nonsense) that rhyme with the word *can*.

18 ©The Mailbox® • *File Folder Centers* • TEC61043

Rings for the King

Identifying rhyming pictures

Preparing the center:

1. Tear out the "Rings for the King" file folder center from the back of the book and the center cards on page 47.

2. Cut out the cards and place them in a resealable plastic bag. Then tape to the bag a copy of the label below. Use a clothespin to attach the bag to the folder.

3. Make a class supply of the take-home practice page on page 20. After a child has had an opportunity to use the center, have her take home a copy of the page to complete with her family.

Using the center:

1. A child places each card faceup.

2. She chooses a card. She says the word *king* and then the name of the picture on the card.

3. If the two words rhyme, she places the card on the king's robe. If they don't, she places the card in a separate pile.

4. She repeats Steps 2 and 3 for each remaining card.

5. She flips all of the cards over to check her answers. If each card from the mat has a king on the back, she is finished. If not, she rearranges the cards until they are placed correctly.

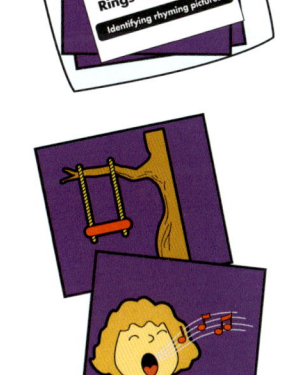

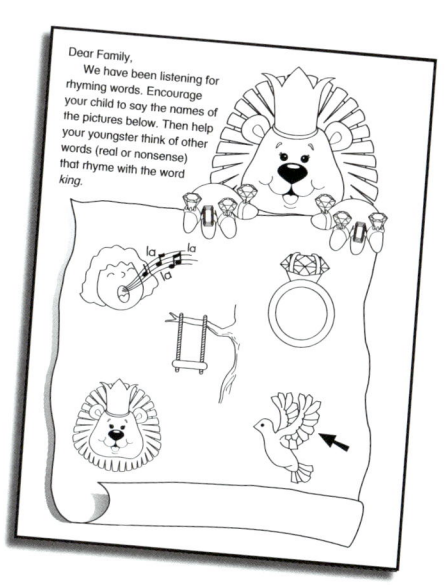

For added fun:

Place at the center a jewelry box filled with several jumbo plastic rings (or short, construction paper strips taped to resemble rings). Each time the child places a card on the mat, invite her to take a ring and place it on one of her fingers. When she has finished the center, encourage her to wiggle her fingers to show off her rings and then place them back in the jewelry box for the next child.

Bag Label

Rings for the King

Identifying rhyming pictures

TEC61043

©The Mailbox® • File Folder Centers • TEC61043

Dear Family,

   We have been listening for rhyming words. Encourage your child to say the names of the pictures below. Then help your youngster think of other words (real or nonsense) that rhyme with the word *king*.

20

©The Mailbox® • *File Folder Centers* • TEC61043

Sailing Seals

Beginning sound /s/

Preparing the center:

1. Tear out the "Sailing Seals" file folder center from the back of the book and the center cards on page 49.

2. Cut out the cards and place them in a resealable plastic bag. Then tape to the bag a copy of the label below. Use a clothespin to attach the bag to the folder.

3. Make a class supply of the take-home practice page on page 22. After a child has had an opportunity to use the center, have him take home a copy of the page to complete with his family.

Using the center:

1. A child places each card faceup.

2. He chooses a card and names the picture.

3. He decides whether the picture's name begins with /s/ like the word *sail*. If it does, he places the card on the sail. If it doesn't, he places it in a separate pile.

4. He repeats Steps 2 and 3 for each remaining card.

5. He flips all of the cards over to check his answers. If each card from the mat has a seal on the back, he returns the cards to the bag. If not, he rearranges the cards until they are placed correctly.

For added fun:

Place a large cardboard tube at the center to resemble a spyglass. Encourage the youngster to complete the center as described above, using his spyglass to locate each card before placing it in the proper location.

Bag Label

Sailing Seals
Beginning sound /s/

TEC61043

©The Mailbox® • File Folder Centers • TEC61043

Dear Family,
    We have been listening for the sound of the letter *s.* Help your child say the name of each picture above, emphasizing the /s/ sound at the beginning of each name. Then invite your youngster to color the page.

Mail for Monkey

Beginning sound /m/

Preparing the center:

1. Tear out the "Mail for Monkey" file folder center from the back of the book and the center cards on page 51.

2. Cut out the cards and place them in a resealable plastic bag. Then tape to the bag a copy of the label below. Use a clothespin to attach the bag to the folder.

3. Make a class supply of the take-home practice page on page 24. After a child has had an opportunity to use the center, have her take home a copy of the page to complete with her family.

Using the center:

1. A child places each picture card faceup.

2. She chooses a card and names the picture. Then she decides whether the picture's name begins with /m/ like the word *mail*. If it does, she places the card on the mailbox. If it doesn't, she places it in a separate pile.

3. She repeats Step 2 for each remaining card.

4. She flips all the cards over to check her answers. If each card on the mat has a mailbox on the back, she is finished. If not, she rearranges the cards until they are placed correctly.

For added fun:

When a youngster is finished with the center, encourage her to dictate a letter to the monkey as you write her words on a sheet of paper. Have her seal her finished letter in an envelope and then place it on the monkey's mailbox. Now he has more mail!

Bag Label

Mail for Monkey

Beginning sound /m/

TEC61043

©The Mailbox® • *File Folder Centers* • TEC61043   23

Dear Family,
   We have been listening for the sound of the letter *m*. Help your child say the names of the pictures below, emphasizing the /m/ sound at the beginning of each name. Then invite your youngster to color the page.

Foxes With Flowers

Beginning sound /f/

Preparing the center:

1. Tear out the "Foxes With Flowers" file folder center from the back of the book and the center cards on page 53.

2. Cut out the cards and place them in a resealable plastic bag. Then tape to the bag a copy of the label below. Use a clothespin to attach the bag to the folder.

3. Make a class supply of the take-home practice page on page 26. After a child has had an opportunity to use the center, have him take home a copy of the page to complete with his family.

Using the center:

1. A child places each card faceup.

2. He chooses a card and names the picture.

3. He decides whether the picture's name begins with /f/ like the word *fox*. If it does, he places the card on the mat. If it doesn't, he places it in a separate pile.

4. He repeats Steps 2 and 3 for each remaining card.

5. He flips all the cards over to check his answers. If each card on the mat has a fox on the back, he is finished. If not, he rearranges the cards until they are placed correctly.

For added fun:

Provide access to an artificial flower with a long stem. When a student is finished with Step 5 (above), have him remove the stacked cards from the mat and place them in a row. Then encourage him to use the artificial flower as a pointer as he names each picture.

Bag Label

Foxes With Flowers
Beginning sound /f/

TEC61043

©The Mailbox • File Folder Centers • TEC61043   25

Dear Family,

We have been listening for the sound of the letter *f*. Help your child say the names of the pictures below, emphasizing the /f/ sound at the beginning of each name. Then invite your youngster to color the page.

Alphabet Soup

Matching identical letters

Preparing the center:

1. Tear out the "Alphabet Soup" file folder center from the back of the book and the center cards on page 55.

2. Cut out the cards and place them in a resealable plastic bag. Then tape to the bag a copy of the label below. Use a clothespin to attach the bag to the folder.

3. Make a class supply of the take-home practice page on page 28. After a child has had an opportunity to use the center, have her take home a copy of the page to complete with her family.

Using the center:

1. A child places each card faceup.

2. She chooses a card and then finds its twin.

3. She flips the cards over to check her answer. If the pictures on the backs of the cards match, she places the cards on the mat. If the pictures do not match, she searches for the correct card to make a matching pair. When she finds it, she places both cards on the mat.

4. She repeats Steps 2 and 3 until all the cards are placed on the mat.

For added fun:

Provide access to a container of alphabet-shaped cereal, a small scoop, and a supply of napkins. When a child has completed the center, invite her to take a scoop of cereal for a special treat. Then encourage her to find any matching pairs before nibbling on her snack.

Bag Label

Alphabet Soup

Matching identical letters

TEC61043

Dear Family,
   We have been matching letters. Help your youngster draw a line from each letter on the left to its twin on the right.

C	A
A	C
B	T
T	B

File Folder Centers Checklist

Student	Underwater Wonders Counting to 5; counting to 10	Swamp Serenade Matching one to one	Bears in the Air Sorting by color	A Growing Garden Ordering by size	Fresh Fixings Copying simple patterns	Midday Munchies Sorting shapes	Pretty Painters Identifying rhyming pictures	Rings for the King Identifying rhyming pictures	Sailing Seals Beginning sound /s/	Mail for Monkey Beginning sound /m/	Foxes With Flowers Beginning sound /f/	Alphabet Soup Matching identical letters
1.												
2.												
3.												
4.												
5.												
6.												
7.												
8.												
9.												
10.												
11.												
12.												
13.												
14.												
15.												
16.												
17.												
18.												
19.												
20.												
21.												
22.												
23.												
24.												
25.												

Student Award
Use at the conclusion of the center activities.

Congratulations!

_____

has worked hard to complete all of our literacy and math centers!

©The Mailbox® • File Folder Centers • TEC61043

Congratulations!

_____

has worked hard to complete all of our literacy and math centers!

©The Mailbox® • File Folder Centers • TEC61043

Replacement Cards

Use with "Underwater Wonders" on page 5.

Use with "Swamp Serenade" on page 7.

Use with "Bears in the Air" on page 9.

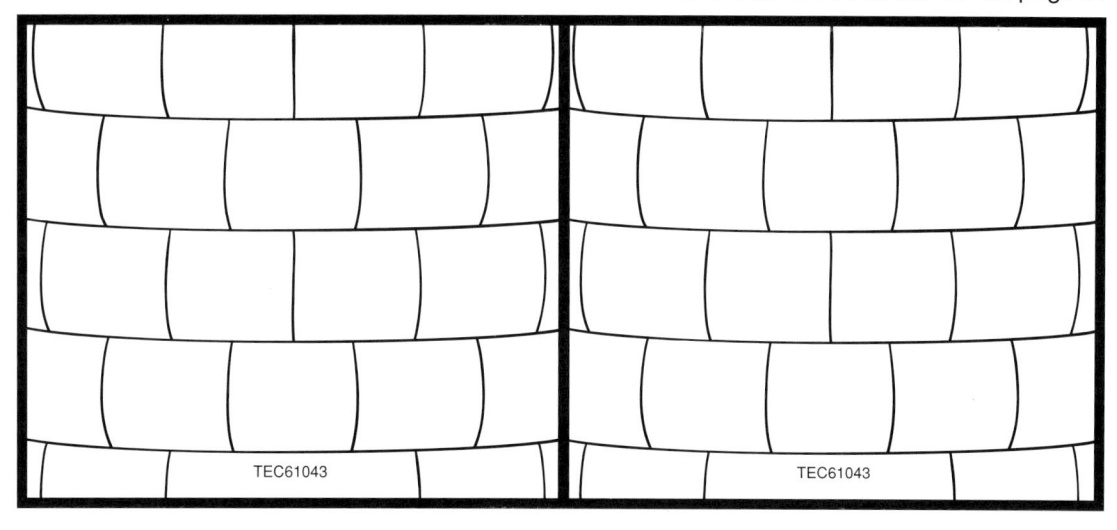

©The Mailbox® • *File Folder Centers* • TEC61043

Replacement Cards
Use with "A Growing Garden" on page 11.

Use with "Fresh Fixings" on page 13.

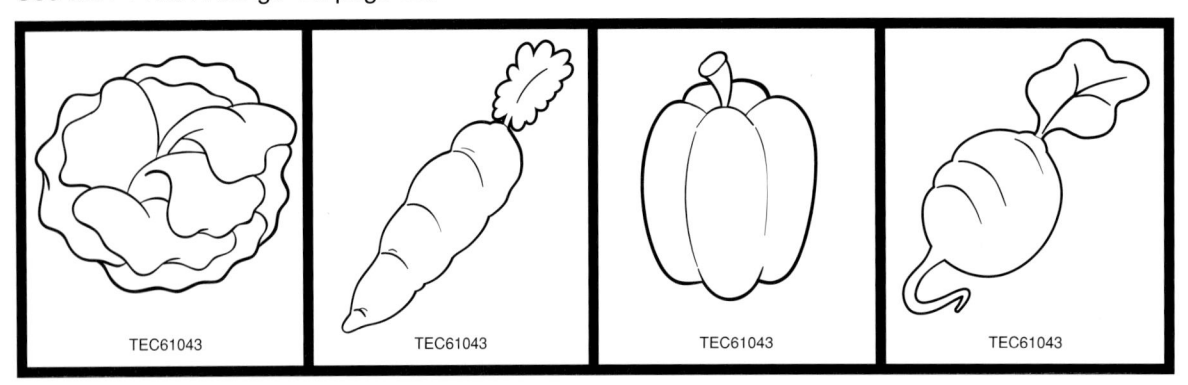

Center Cards
Use with "Underwater Wonders" on page 5.

Underwater Wonders
TEC61043

Underwater Wonders
TEC61043

Underwater Wonders
TEC61043

Underwater Wonders
TEC61043

Underwater Wonders
TEC61043

Underwater Wonders
TEC61043

Underwater Wonders
TEC61043

Underwater Wonders
TEC61043

Underwater Wonders
TEC61043

Underwater Wonders
TEC61043

Center Cards
Use with "Swamp Serenade" on page 7.

Swamp Serenade
TEC61043

Swamp Serenade
TEC61043

Swamp Serenade
TEC61043

Swamp Serenade
TEC61043

Swamp Serenade
TEC61043

Swamp Serenade
TEC61043

Swamp Serenade
TEC61043

Swamp Serenade
TEC61043

Center Cards
Use with "Bears in the Air" on page 9.

Bears in the Air
TEC61043

Bears in the Air
TEC61043

Bears in the Air
TEC61043

Bears in the Air
TEC61043

Bears in the Air
TEC61043

Bears in the Air
TEC61043

Center Cards
Use with "A Growing Garden" on page 11.

©The Mailbox® • *File Folder Centers* • TEC61043

| A Growing Garden
TEC61043 | 4 |
| A Growing Garden
TEC61043 | 3 |
| A Growing Garden
TEC61043 | 2 |
| A Growing Garden
TEC61043 | 1 |

| 1 | A Growing Garden
TEC61043 |
| 2 | A Growing Garden
TEC61043 |
| 3 | A Growing Garden
TEC61043 |
| 4 | A Growing Garden
TEC61043 |

Center Cards
Use with "Fresh Fixings" on page 13.

41
©The Mailbox® • *File Folder Centers* • TEC61043

Fresh Fixings
TEC61043

Fresh Fixings
TEC61043

Fresh Fixings
TEC61043

Fresh Fixings
TEC61043

Fresh Fixings
TEC61043

Fresh Fixings
TEC61043

Fresh Fixings
TEC61043

Fresh Fixings
TEC61043

Fresh Fixings
TEC61043

Fresh Fixings
TEC61043

Fresh Fixings
TEC61043

Fresh Fixings
TEC61043

Center Cards
Use with "Midday Munchies" on page 15.

©The Mailbox® • *File Folder Centers* • TEC61043

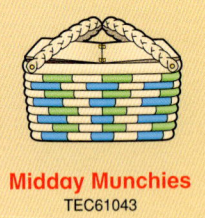

Midday Munchies
TEC61043

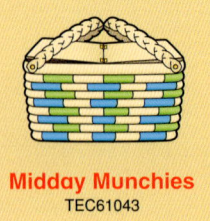

Midday Munchies
TEC61043

Midday Munchies
TEC61043

Midday Munchies
TEC61043

Midday Munchies
TEC61043

Midday Munchies
TEC61043

Center Cards
Use with "Pretty Painters" on page 17.

©The Mailbox® • *File Folder Centers* • TEC61043
45

Pretty Painters
TEC61043

Pretty Painters
TEC61043

Pretty Painters
TEC61043

Pretty Painters
TEC61043

Pretty Painters
TEC61043

Center Cards

Use with "Rings for the King" on page 19.

Rings for the King
TEC61043

Rings for the King
TEC61043

Rings for the King
TEC61043

Rings for the King
TEC61043

Rings for the King
TEC61043

Center Cards
Use with "Sailing Seals" on page 21.

©The Mailbox® • *File Folder Centers* • TEC61043

49

Sailing Seals
TEC61043

Sailing Seals
TEC61043

Sailing Seals
TEC61043

Sailing Seals
TEC61043

Sailing Seals
TEC61043

Sailing Seals
TEC61043

Center Cards
Use with "Mail for Monkey" on page 23.

Mail for Monkey
TEC61043

Mail for Monkey
TEC61043

Mail for Monkey
TEC61043

Mail for Monkey
TEC61043

Mail for Monkey
TEC61043

Mail for Monkey
TEC61043

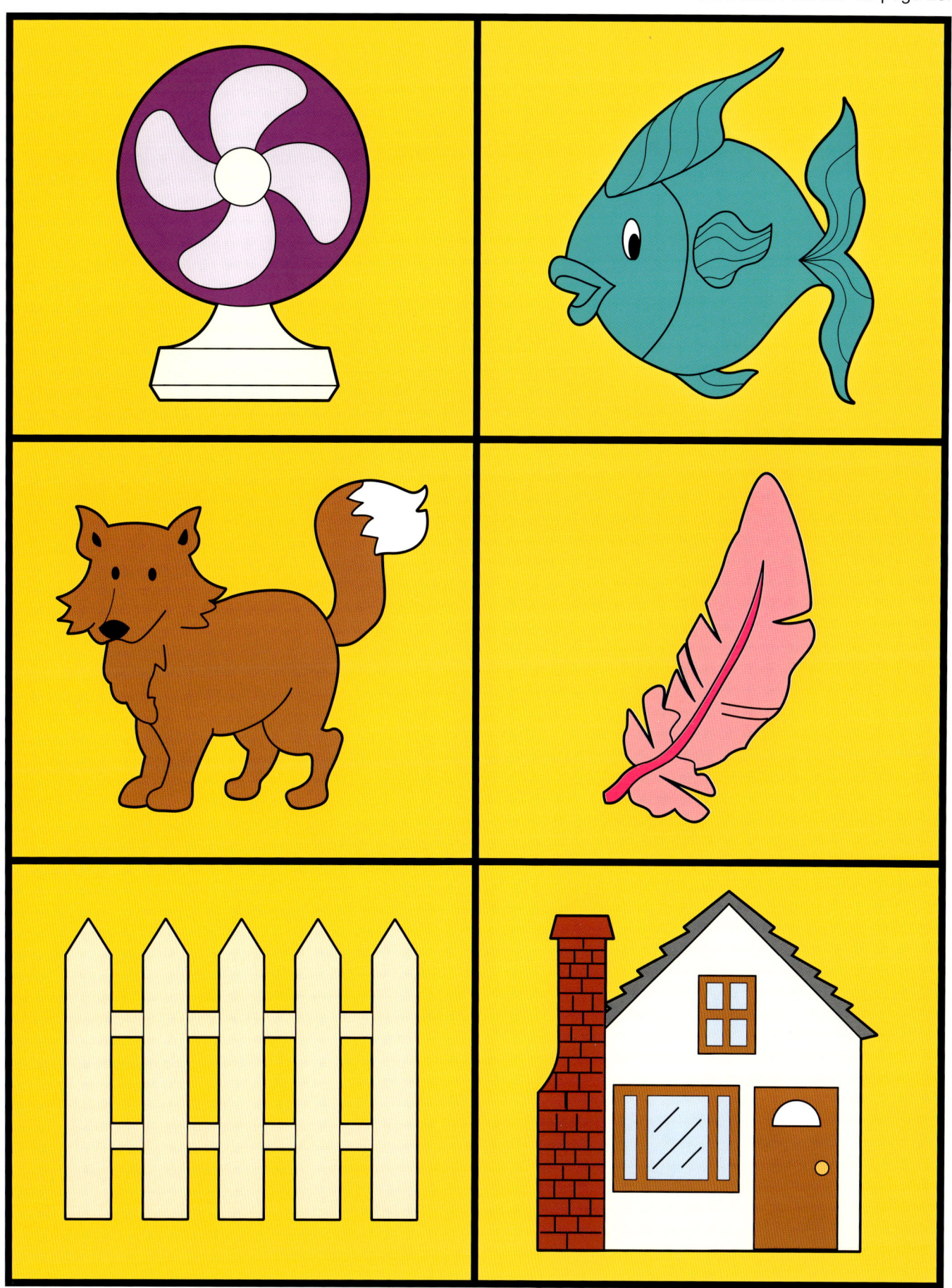

Center Cards
Use with "Foxes With Flowers" on page 25.

©The Mailbox® • *File Folder Centers* • TEC61043

Foxes With Flowers
TEC61043

Foxes With Flowers
TEC61043

Foxes With Flowers
TEC61043

Foxes With Flowers
TEC61043

Foxes With Flowers
TEC61043

Foxes With Flowers
TEC61043

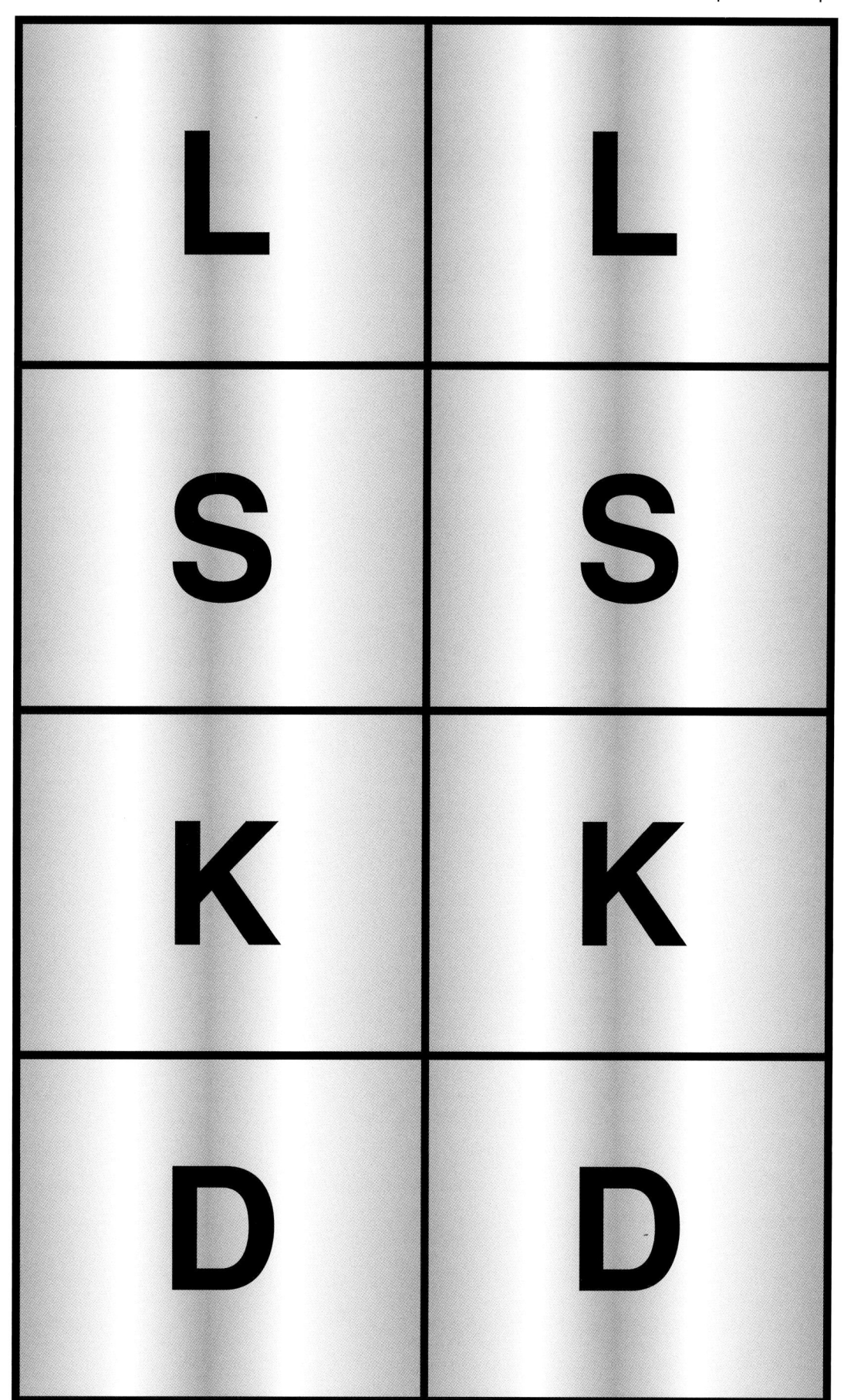

Center Cards
Use with "Alphabet Soup" on page 27.

L	L
S	S
K	K
D	D

©The Mailbox® • *File Folder Centers* • TEC61043

Alphabet Soup
TEC61043

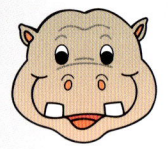

Alphabet Soup
TEC61043

Alphabet Soup
TEC61043

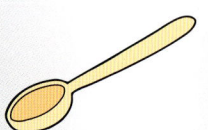

Alphabet Soup
TEC61043

Alphabet Soup
TEC61043

Alphabet Soup
TEC61043

Alphabet Soup
TEC61043

Alphabet Soup
TEC61043

Underwater Wonders

Counting to 5; counting to 10

Inside this folder:

Count.

To find the **cards** for this center, see page 33.

To find the **teacher page** and **take-home practice page,** see pages 5 and 6.

Turn to see the front of the folder.

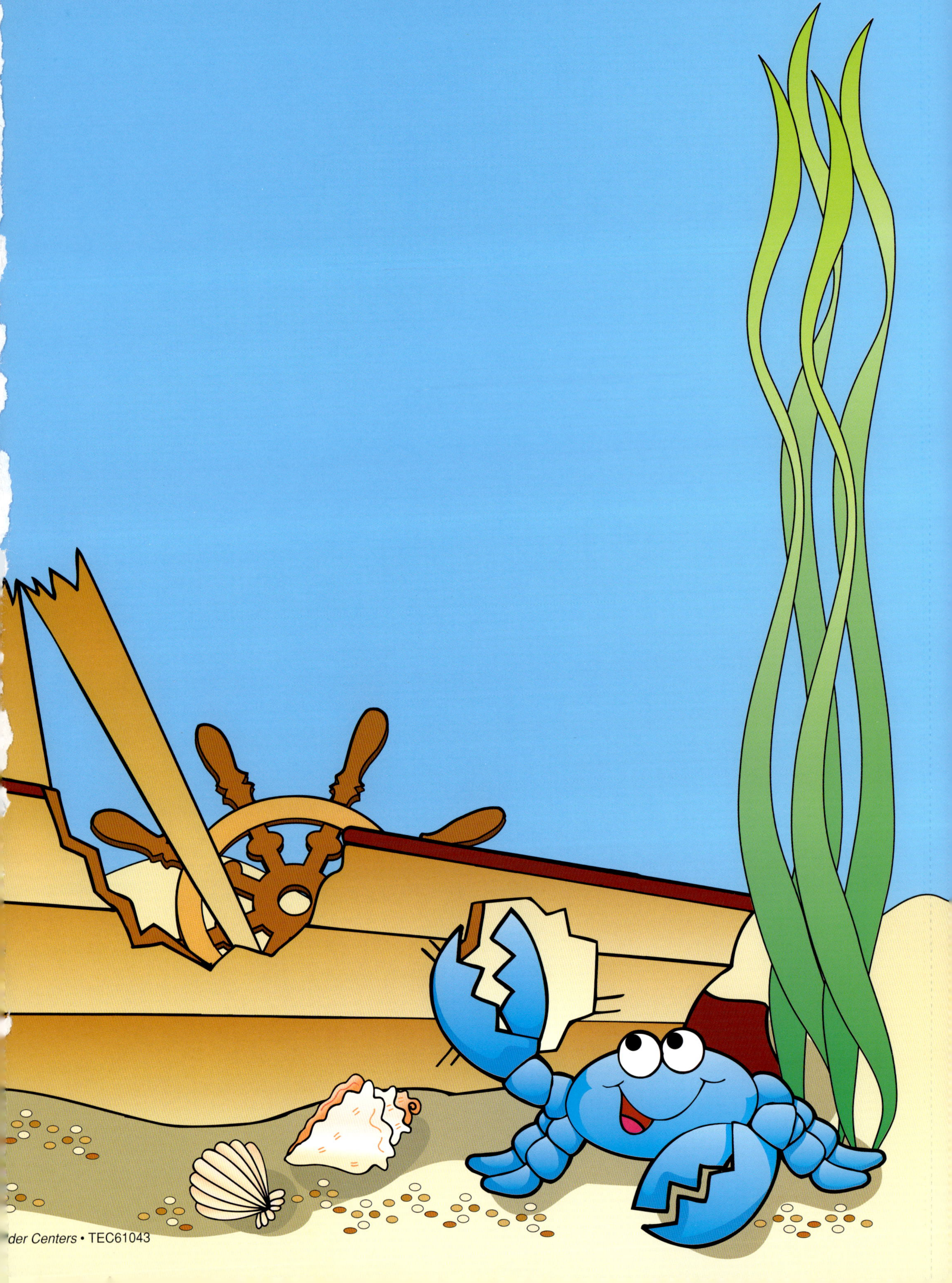

Count.

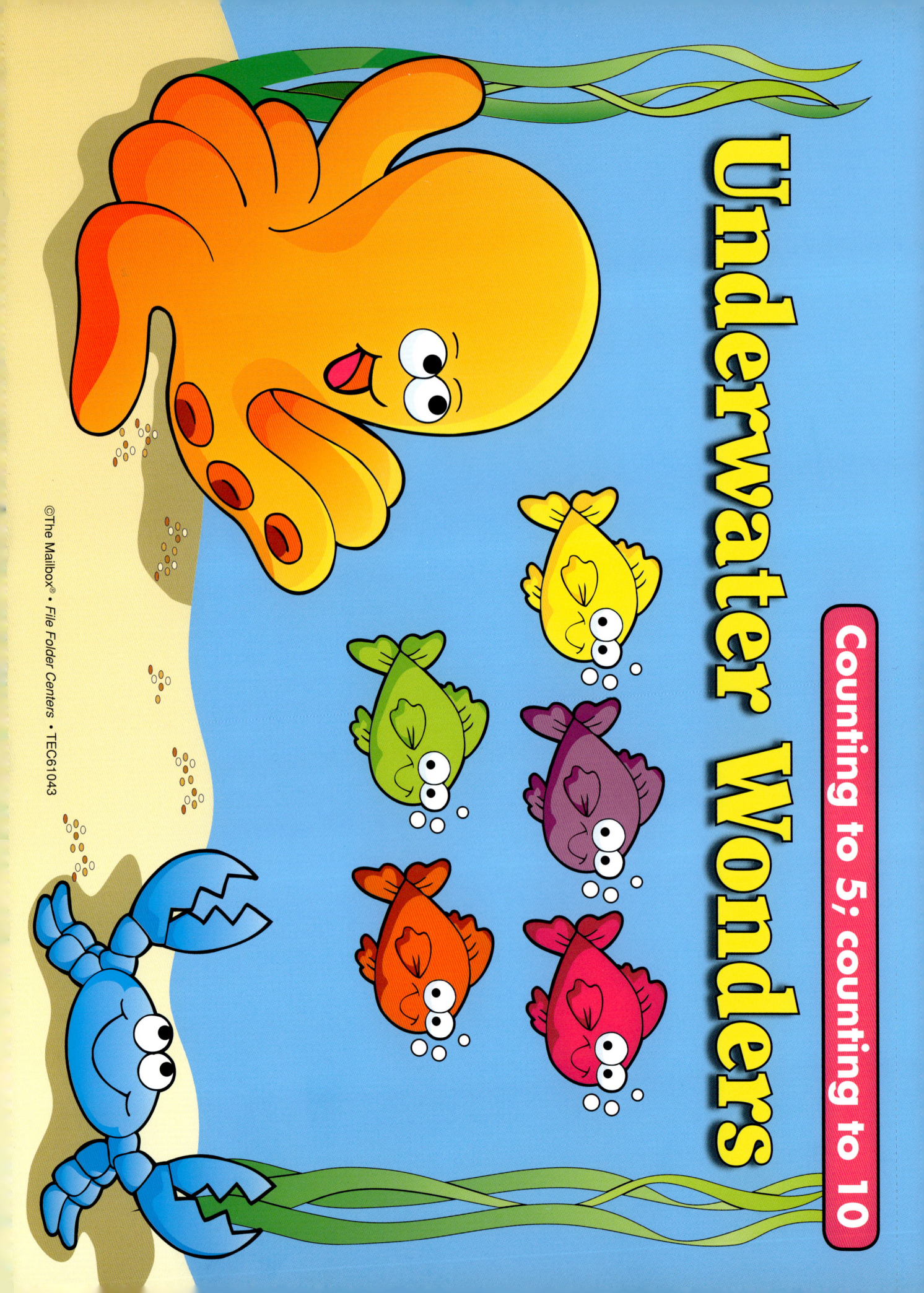

Underwater Wonders

Counting to 5; counting to 10

Swamp Serenade
Matching one to one

Inside this folder:

Place.

To find the **cards** for this center, see page 35.

To find the **teacher page** and the **take-home practice page,** see pages 7 and 8.

Turn to see the front of the folder.

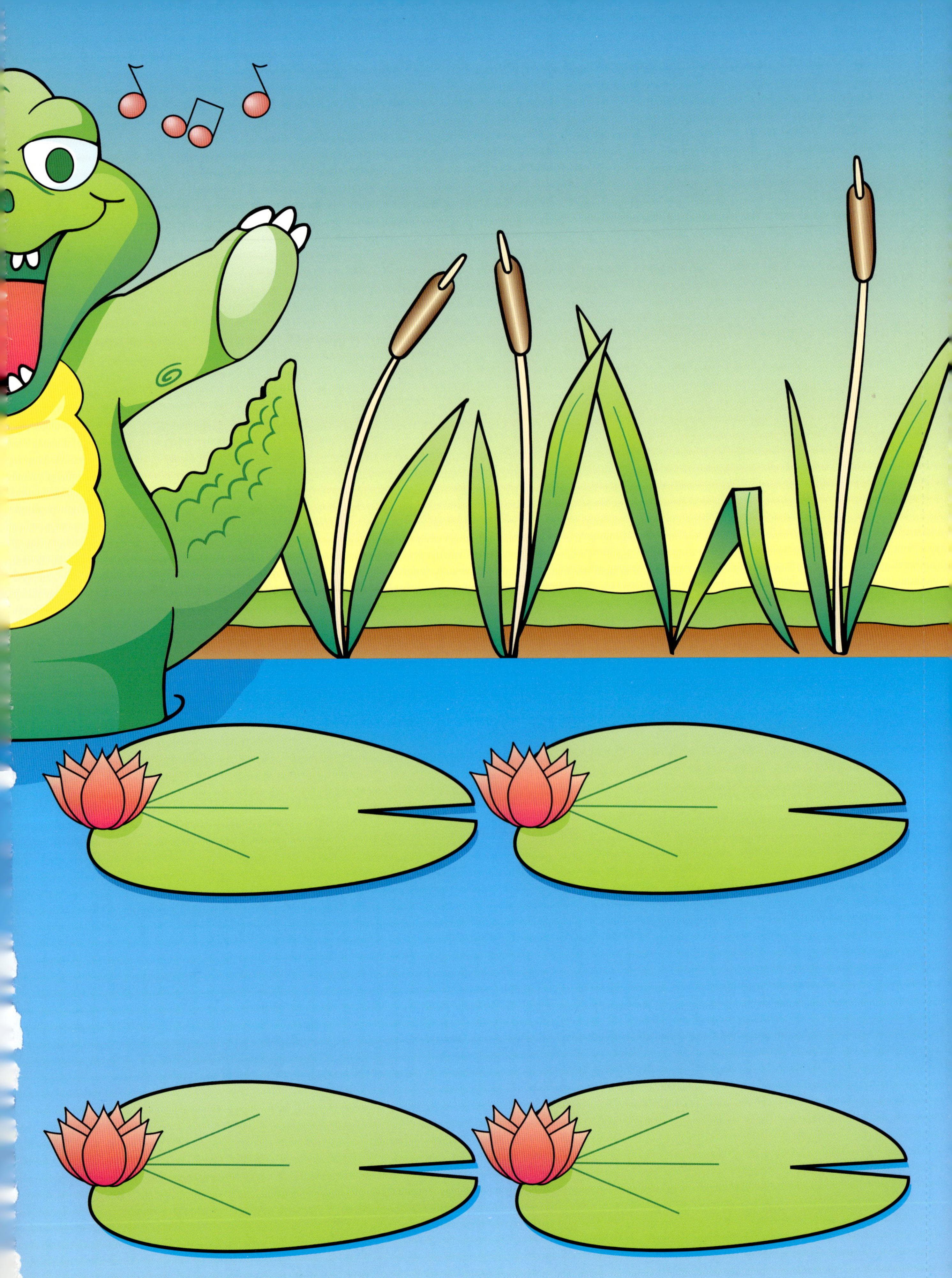

Place.

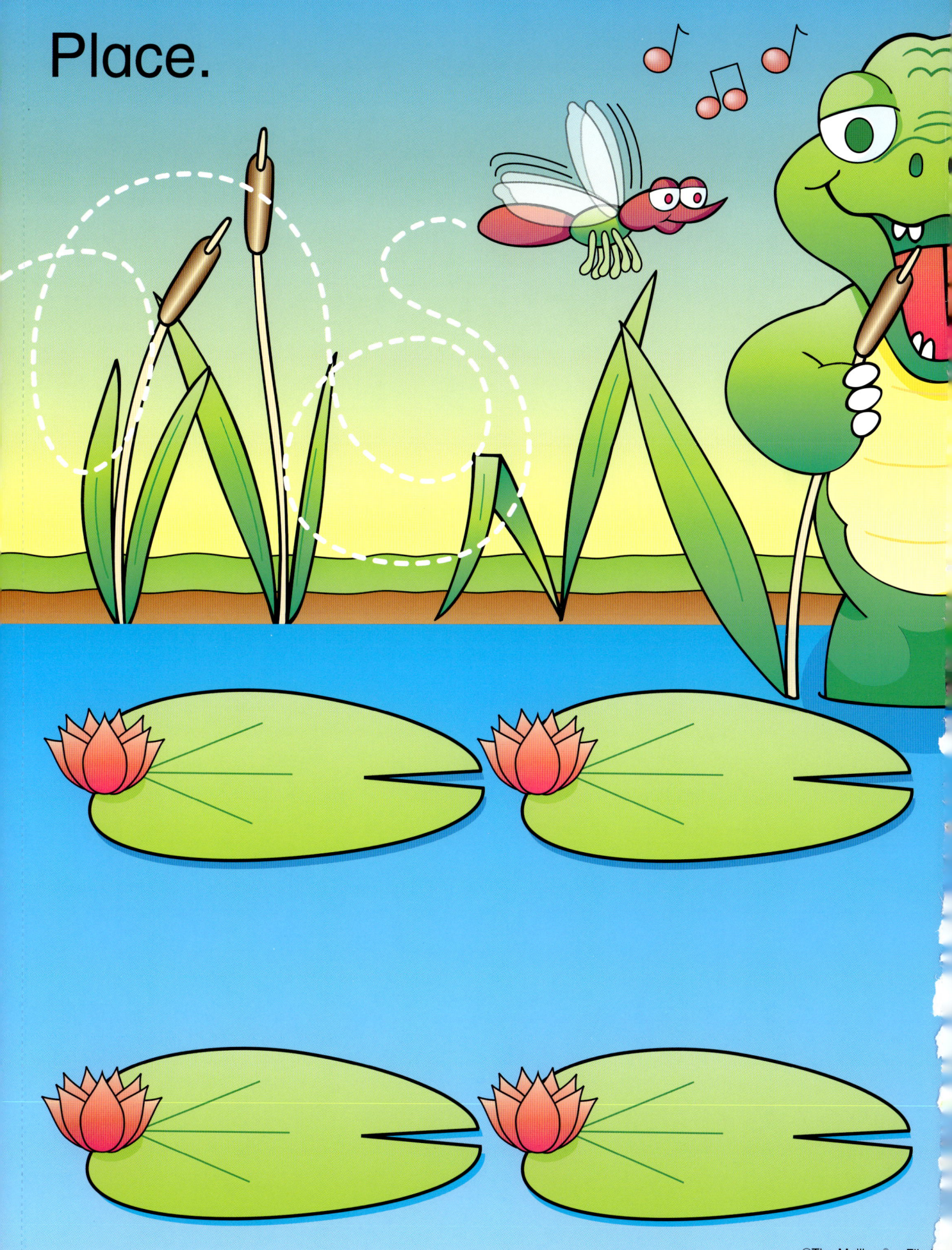

Swamp Serenade

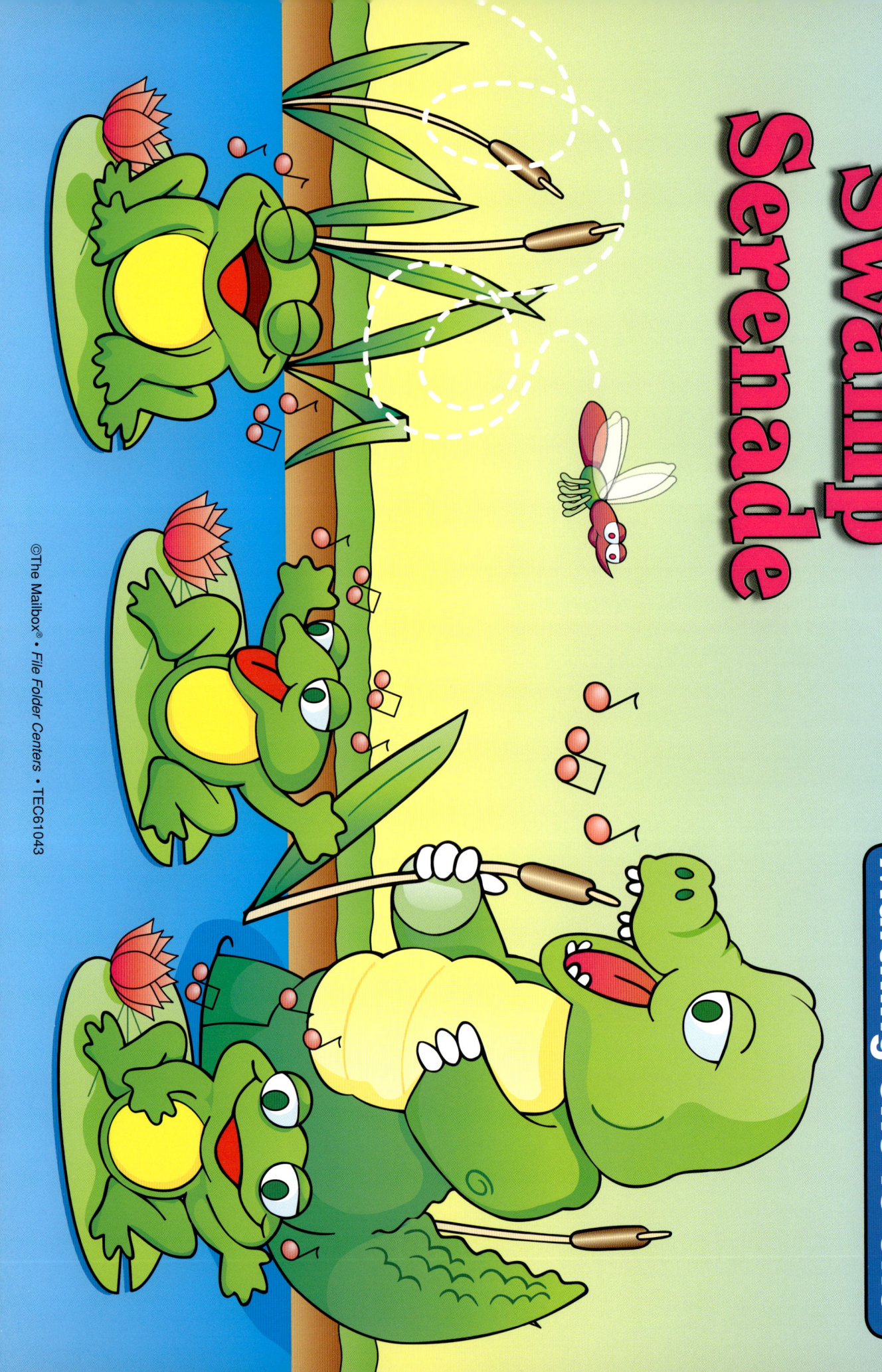

Matching one to one

©The Mailbox® • File Folder Centers • TEC61043

Bears in the Air
Sorting by color

Inside this folder:

Sort.

To find the **cards** for this center, see page 37.

To find the **teacher page** and **take-home practice page,** see pages 9 and 10.

Turn to see the front of the folder. →

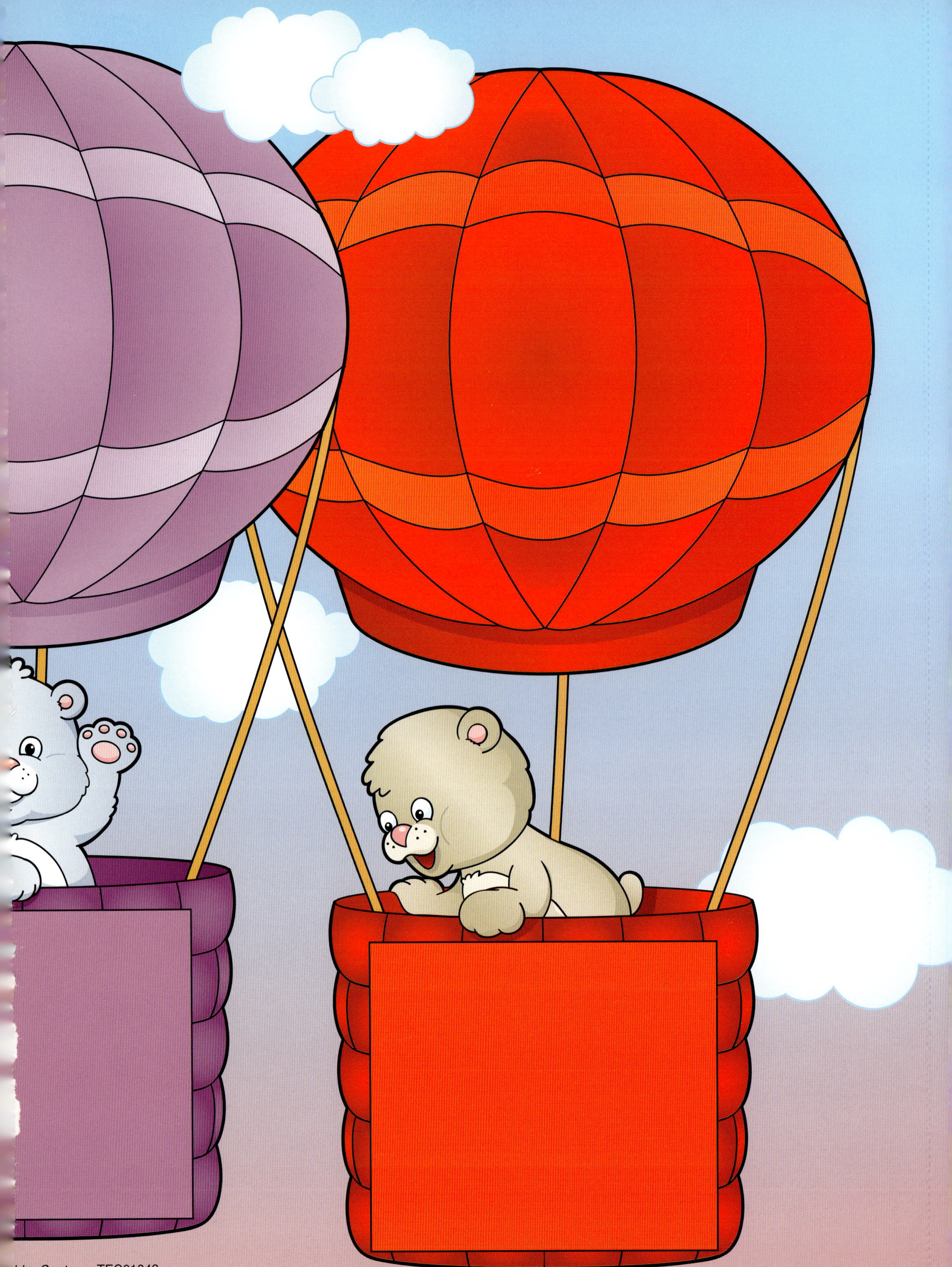

Sort.

Bears in the Air

Sorting by color

A Growing Garden
Ordering by size

Inside this folder:

Place.

To find the **cards** for this center, see page 39.

To find the **teacher page** and the **take-home practice page,** see pages 11 and 12.

Turn to see the front of the folder.

der Centers • TEC61043

Place.

A Growing Garden

Ordering by size

Fresh Fixings

Copying simple patterns

Inside this folder:

Place.
Say.
Match.

To find the **cards** for this center, see page 41.

To find the **teacher page** and the **take-home practice page,** see pages 13 and 14.

Turn to see the front of the folder.

Place.
Say.
Match.

Rabbit Ranch Dressing

©The Mailbox® • *File Folder Centers* • TEC61043

Fresh Fixings

Copying simple patterns

Midday Munchies
Sorting shapes

Inside this folder:

Sort.

To find the **cards** for this center, see page 43.

To find the **teacher page** and **take-home practice page,** see pages 15 and 16.

Turn to see the front of the folder.

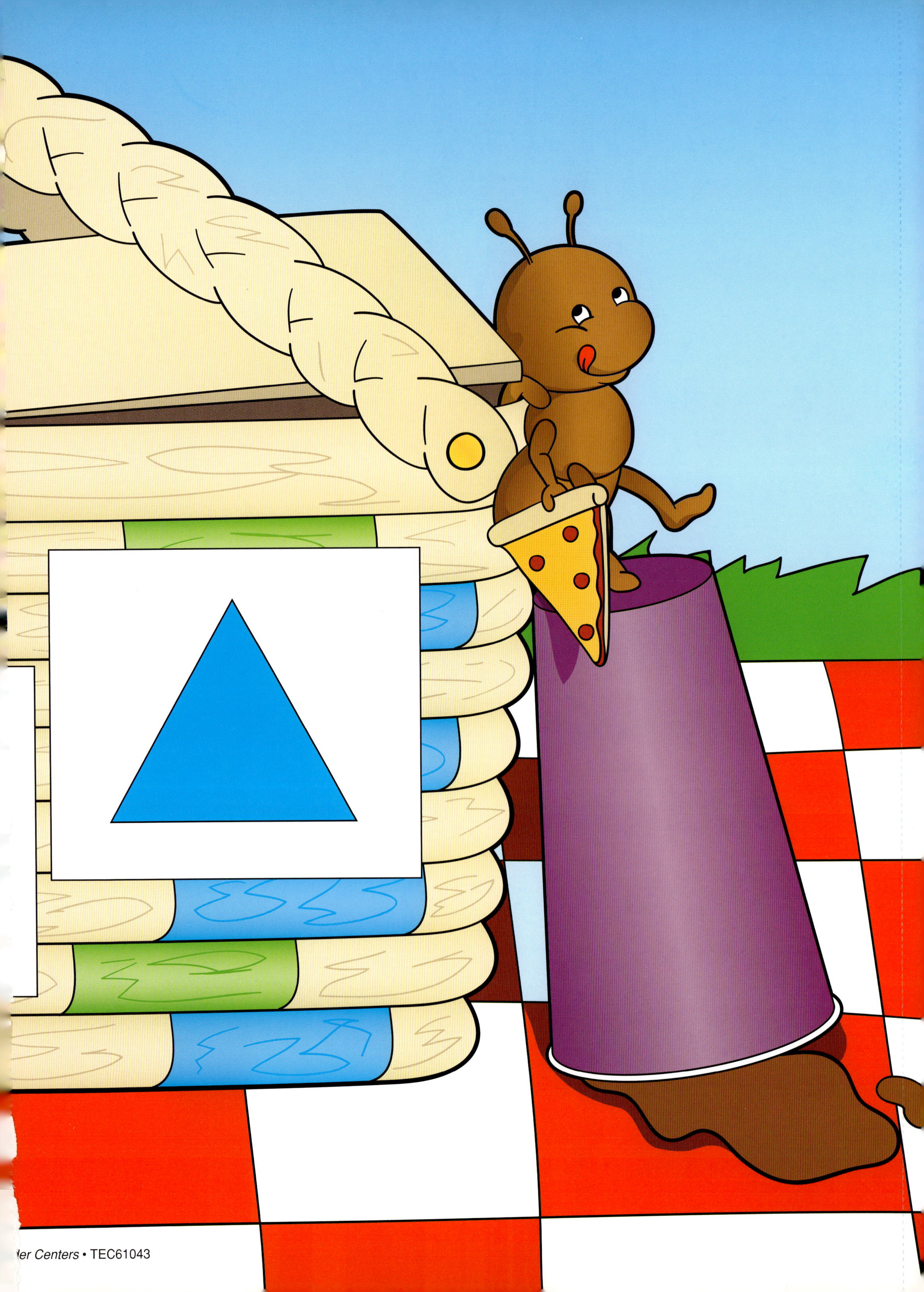

Sort.

Midday Munchies

Sorting shapes

Pretty Painters

Identifying rhyming pictures

Inside this folder:

Choose.
Say.
Place.

To find the **cards** for this center, see page 45.

To find the **teacher page** and **take-home practice page,** see pages 17 and 18.

Turn to see the front of the folder.

Choose.
Say.
Place.

©The Mailbox® • File Folder Centers • TEC61043

Pretty Painters

Identifying rhyming pictures

Rings for the King
Identifying rhyming pictures

Inside this folder:

Choose.
Say.
Place.

To find the **cards** for this center, see page 47.

To find the **teacher page** and **take-home practice page,** see pages 19 and 20.

Turn to see the front of the folder.

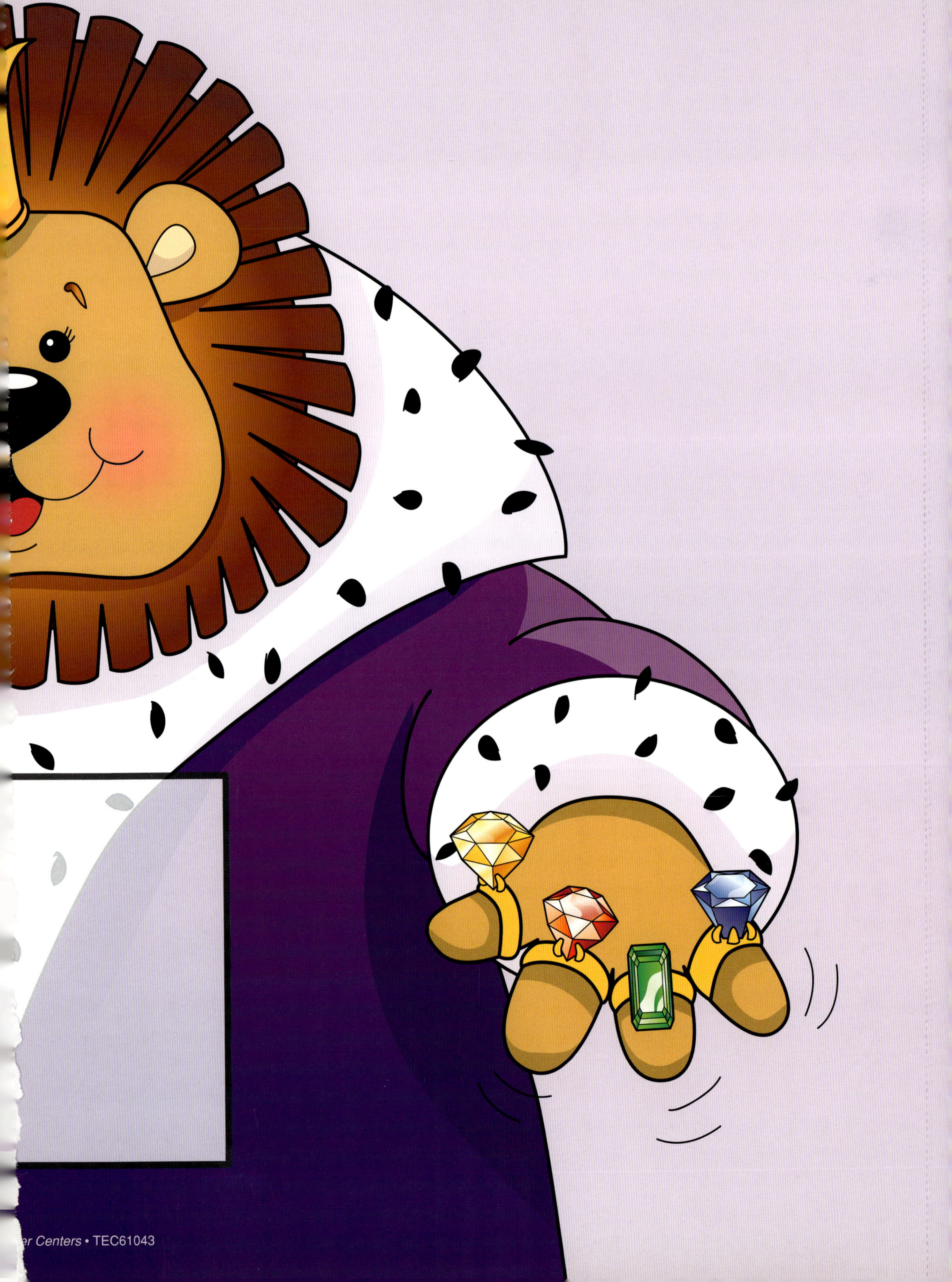

Choose.
Say.
Place.

Rings for the King

Identifying rhyming pictures

Sailing Seals
Beginning sound /s/

Inside this folder:

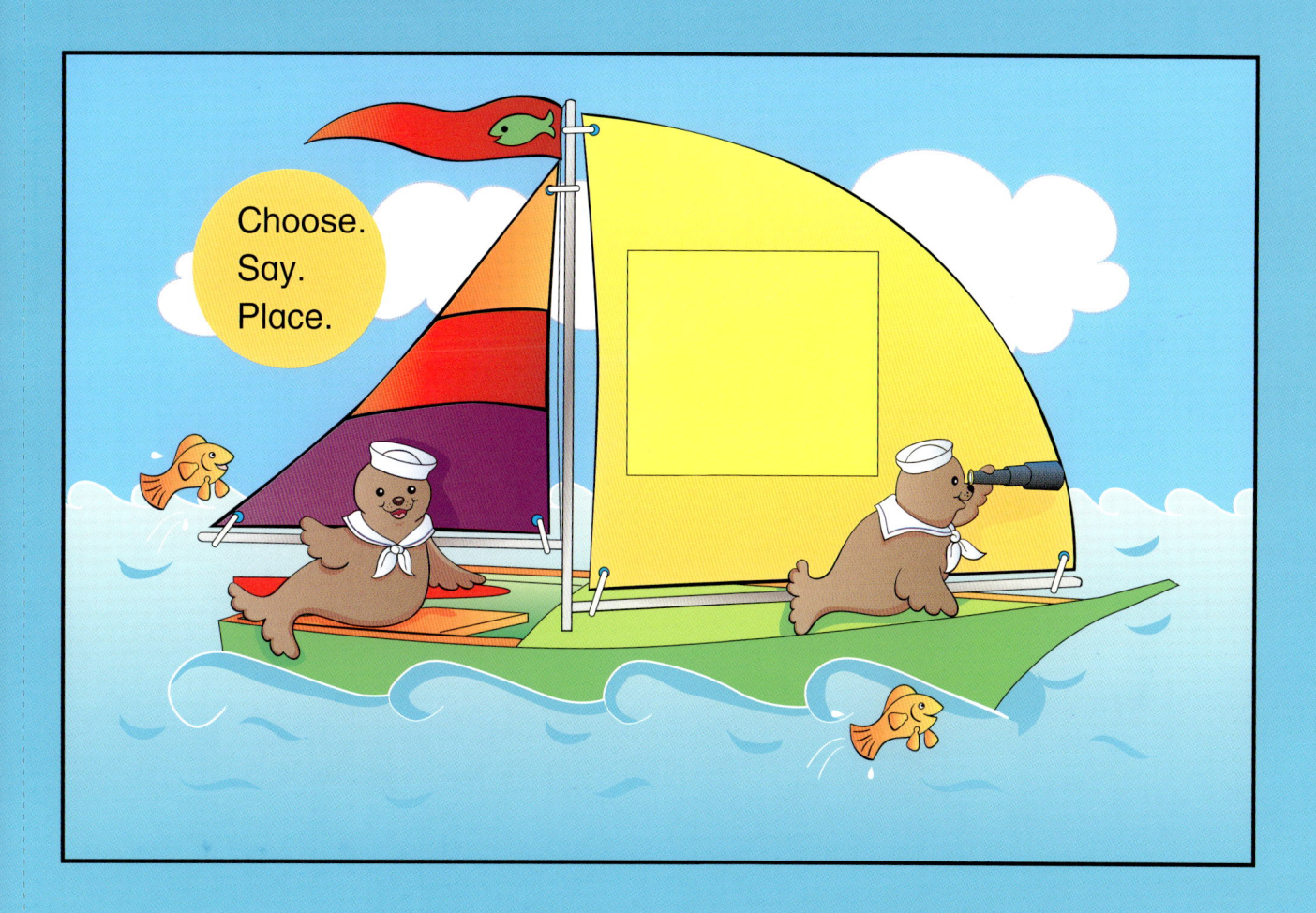

Choose. Say. Place.

To find the **cards** for this center, see page 49.

To find the **teacher page** and **take-home practice page,** see pages 21 and 22.

Turn to see the front of the folder. ➡

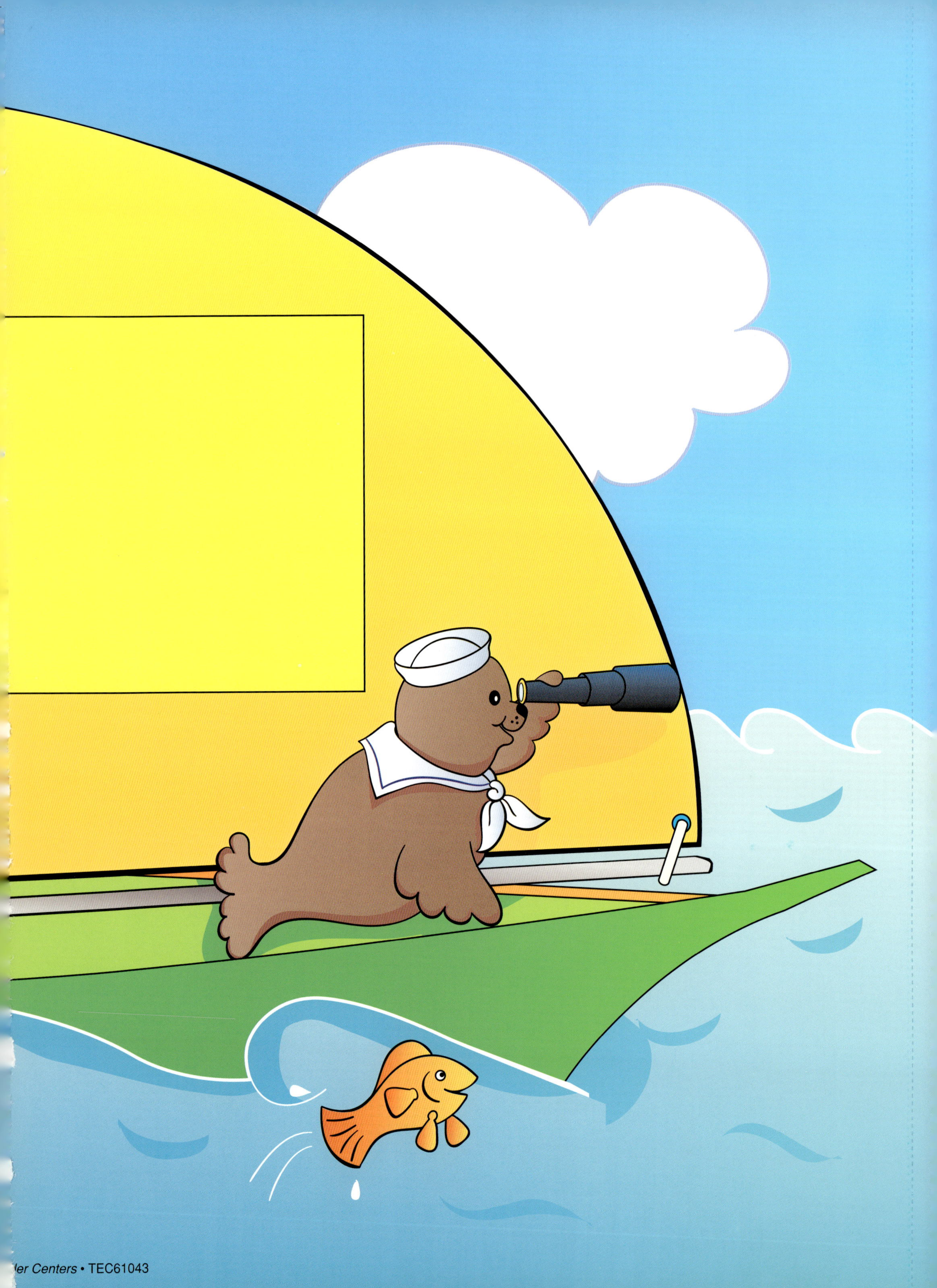

Choose. Say. Place.

Sailing Seals

Beginning sound /s/

Mail for Monkey
Beginning sound /m/

Inside this folder:

Place.

To find the **cards** for this center, see page 51.

To find the **teacher page** and **take-home practice page,** see pages 23 and 24.

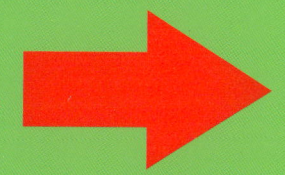

Turn to see the front of the folder.

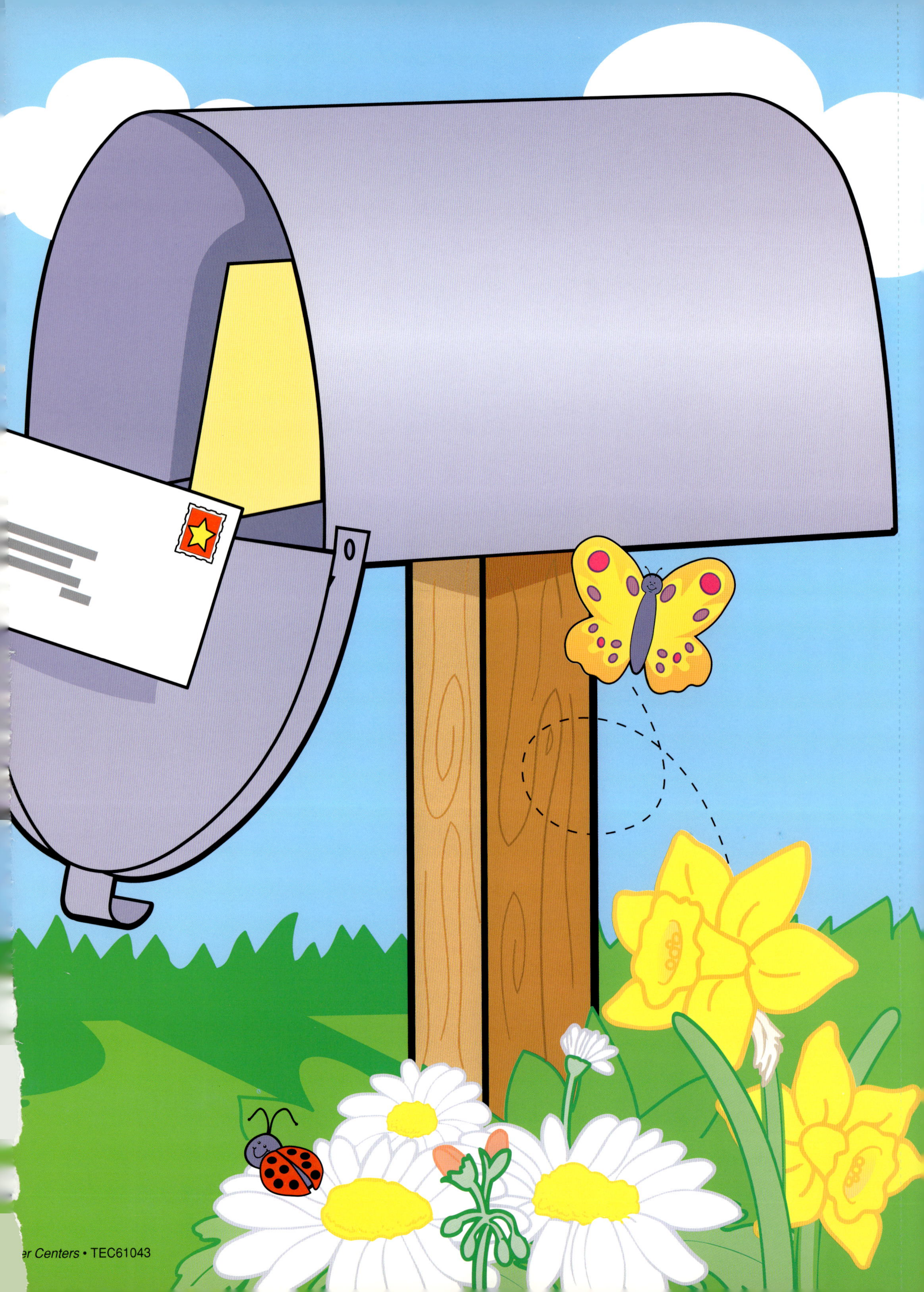

Place.

Mail for Monkey

Beginning sound /m/

Foxes With Flowers

Beginning sound /f/

Inside this folder:

Choose.
Say.
Place.

To find the **cards** for this center, see page 53.

To find the **teacher page** and **take-home practice page,** see pages 25 and 26.

Turn to see the front of the folder.

Choose.
Say.
Place.

©The Mailbox® • *File Folder Centers* • TEC61043

Foxes With Flowers

Beginning sound /f/